I0450067

Mama, Please Don't Sentence Me to Die

by
Doris Head

Bloomington, IN  Milton Keynes, UK

authorHOUSE®

AuthorHouse™
1663 Liberty Drive, Suite 200
Bloomington, IN 47403
www.authorhouse.com
Phone: 1-800-839-8640

AuthorHouse™ UK Ltd.
500 Avebury Boulevard
Central Milton Keynes, MK9 2BE
www.authorhouse.co.uk
Phone: 08001974150

First published by AuthorHouse 4/12/2007

ISBN: 978-1-4259-9756-4 (sc)

*Printed in the United States of America
Bloomington, Indiana*

This book is printed on acid-free paper.

Dedication

To my four sons: Mike, Kent, Chris, and Mark; my four granddaughters: Bridget, Brittany, Chealsea, and little Doris; my sister, brothers, sisters-in-law, and brothers-in-law; my nieces, nephews, cousins, friends, and all people around the world—I pray that we can come together in prayer each day for the unborn.

Table of Cotents

Dedication   v

Forward   ix

Chapter 1
My First Hearing of Miscarriages and Abortions   1

Chapter 2
Mama Please Don't Sentence Me to Die:
The Voice of the Unborn Revealed by God   5

Chapter 3
God Worked It All Out   9

Chapter 4
Calling All Ladies: Please Listen Up   13

Chapter 5
I Learned How to Lean and Depend on Jesus   17

Chapter 6
Mommy Please Don't Sentence Me to Die   21

Words of Thanks   25

About the Author   27

Forward

Ever since I was a young child about the age of nine, I always loved to read and write. My favorite books are the Bible, and health and Black history books. Some of my favorite writings were poems, songs, plays, and short stories. I never really did anything with them, so I just threw them away, but I always had a desire to write about something worthwhile. I knew in my heart that I wanted to write a book and have it published. I never really knew anything about writing or publishing a book, so all my writing would go in the trash. I'm glad to say that here I am, forty years later, with a greater desire to write.

In April of 2005, around Easter, I began to pray for God to help me with the desires of my heart. I would pray about it, then some nights I might forget about it. One night in May of 2006, I was at my job, standing at my workstation, when I had one of the most unusual experiences I had ever had in my life. As I stood there working, all of a sudden, I heard a little voice in my head. The little voice that I heard sounded so tiny, so sweet, and so heavenly, but yet so real. I couldn't believe I was hearing this; it was like a baby talking to its mother. The baby was begging its mother to please let her live: "Please don't sentence me to die."

There were two women standing not that far from me, and then right out of the blue I went to them and asked them about publishing a book. Neither one knew anything about publishing a book, and they gave me a very weird look when I asked them. I then went back to work, but I could still hear that little voice in my head, so I went to the restroom. When I stepped into the restroom, I asked myself, "What's going on?" I thought it might be that the medication I was taking had me hearing things. As I stared at myself in the mirror, I began to wash my face, and I returned back to work. I didn't hear any more voices until I got home around midnight. I did as I usually do and began getting ready for bed; as I was sitting on the edge of the bed, I began to hear the little voice again. It was the same conversation: a baby pleading for her life. The baby was begging her mother to please let her live. I continued to hear this voice off and on for about two weeks, until one night, I heard a different voice. This voice told me to write a book, because it was my time. I was wondering what was going on, but being an obedient child of God, I began to write. I began jotting down on a piece of paper the conversation I had heard that day on my job. Earlier that morning, I was awakened by a mother's voice at my bedroom door; it was my granddaughter Bridget.

She said, "Grandma?"

I replied with "Huh?"

After I replied, I didn't hear anything else, so I got out of the bed. To my surprise, there was no one at the door. I told one of the ladies I had talked to earlier on the job that I kept hearing voices and I was writing a book. I said, "A voice said write, so that's what I'm going to do." Farther on in the book, you will read about how I got published and started my journey. I'm praying that the readers of this book will help save a dying future. Why destroy the future of tomorrow today?

Chapter 1

My First Hearing of Miscarriages and Abortions

When I was about the age of fourteen, I would always hear older ladies talking about someone who had had a miscarriage. I didn't even know what that meant at the time; see, I'm from the old school, and they didn't tell you to much of anything back then. Anything that had to do with sex you would have to learn from the older girls at school or maybe a book that would get passed around in school. One day, I asked this girl what the word miscarriage meant. She said it was when a woman got pregnant and something went wrong in the pregnancy and caused the baby to die. I said, "Stop lying, girl, I can't believe little babies die." I really didn't like that answer, and I couldn't accept the fact that a little baby could die before it was born. So when I got home from school, I built up enough nerve to ask my mother what miscarriage meant.

She said, "And why do you want to know that?" I explained to her that I had overheard her talking to a lady about this other lady who had had a miscarriage. I had asked a girl at school and she had said it was when the baby died before it was born. Mama said, "That's about right; something goes wrong and it causes the lady to lose the baby."

"Go wrong," I said, "what you mean go wrong?"

Mama said, "The lady might fall, lift something too heavy, or maybe her body isn't strong enough to carry a baby. Sometimes, women decide they don't want their babies and they do something to themselves to make them lose their babies." I continued to ask questions, and Mama said, "There you go again with all those questions." I just wanted to know how anyone could be so cruel to an innocent unborn child. Mom said she had heard of people drinking different kinds of oil to do harm to a baby. She said, "That's hearsay; I can't prove it, because I had all eight of y'all." One Sunday I was in church and the preacher's text was about killing babies, but he was using a word I had never heard before; it was abortion. This was back when I was still a teenager; my curiosity ran wild out of everything he said; all I could remember was the word abortion. The next day, I went to school and asked this girl if she knew what the word abortion meant.

She said, "Yeah, it's when a woman gets pregnant and doesn't want her baby, and she goes to a doctor and they kill the baby." I couldn't imagine anyone killing a little baby; I was very disturbed by what she had said. From then on, I always wondered what I could do to help stop abortions. Now here I am, nearly forty-five year later, still trying to figure it out. I'm praying that the contents of this book can change someone's mind and heart about her unborn child. If it only saves one unborn child, then heaven will rejoice. Just think about it—this is a very painful death for any unborn child. Do you really believe in God? God is not pleased with this kind of thing; please do not allow your unborn child to die. Someone will be happy to adopt your child; please have a change of heart. Let the babies grow up to be boys and girls, young men and women. You never know what the future holds for your children—they may become doctors, lawyers, presidents, senators, preachers, and prophets.

I was talking to this lady about abortions, and she said, "I don't see what the big deal is about abortions; they're legal."

I said, "Just because it's legal by people doesn't mean it's right. What seems right to people is not always pleasing to God." -Whatever your problem may be, just seek the highest power (God). He is Jehovah God; please don't allow this to happen. It's was wrong in the past, it's wrong now, and it will be wrong in the future. You can't connect three wrongs together and make it right. So regardless of how it's said, how it's done, and how it's studied, it's wrong. So, ladies, let's get involved to help stop the killing of babies. Men, you can help, too, because if there's a baby, there's a father. Just think about it; babies are our future.

Chapter 2

Mama Please Don't Sentence Me to Die: The Voice of the Unborn Revealed by God

Dear Mama, I heard you talking on the telephone; you were speaking with your best friend; you told her you were almost five months pregnant with me. Mama, you said you didn't have time for a baby, that I would only be in your way. You told your friend that you knew that I was a little girl, but I would never live in your world. Please, Mama, don't sentence me to die. You discussed the day and time; you knew the exact hour that I was scheduled to be aborted. When you said those words, I began to move; you went on to say in a few weeks it would all be over. Please, Mama, don't sentence me to die. Mama, Grandma didn't abort you; why can't you understand I want to live, too? Please, Mama, don't sentence me to die. Mama, I haven'-

done anything wrong, and I promise I will never make you cry. Please, Mama, don't sentence me to die. Let me grow up to be your little girl; I'll take care of you, Mama, when you grow old. I want to live; I know it's God's will. You will never know how beautiful I will be or see me pull the lights off the Christmas tree; you will never see me wear my little yellow dress or hear Grandma say, "She's a mess."

Please, Mama, don't sentence me to death. Mama, God knew me before I was formed in your womb. It's not God's will to destroy the unborn babies. I have never done wrong; why should the innocent babies have to die in such a painful way? My little body is flesh and blood, and I have already developed a brain, Mama; do you realize I will feel so much pain? Mama, don't sentence me to die. If you just can't change your mind, I will be with Jesus; I will be just fine. If you allow me to die, please bury my little body, but don't you cry; underneath the green grass is where I will be, until Jesus comes and sets me free. Jesus will then give me a beautiful name, Mama; do you know what it might be? Read Mark 5: 41 and you will see my name and the meaning of it. Please, Mama, don't sentence me to die. Well, Mama, the time and the hour is almost here, but as I begin to move, you begin to pray. You are praying to the highest power—that is God. I heard you say, "Father, please forgive me; why am I planning to abort my baby? Father, I know this is not your will; I need my little girl. Father God, I have changed my mind; I want my baby to live. Amen."

Thank you, Mama, for having a changed mind and heart; maybe it wasn't your will but surely it was God's. Thanks, Mama, for taking me off death row. Praise God you didn't let me die. Now I can relax in my bed (your womb) until my arrival, which will be soon. You will be so happy when you see my little face; just hold and hug me, then sing "Amazing Grace." Grandma will be waiting to hold me in her arms; she will kiss my cheeks and say, "What a little charm." I'm getting a little sleepy now; its been a long day. It's time for me to take a nap. I will see you in a few weeks, Mama; my bed will then be your lap. I love you, Mama—your unborn baby.

The story you have just finished reading was the conversation I could hear in my head, the most beautiful little voice I ever heard, pleading for her life. Will you take just a few minutes to visualize anyone pleading for their lives? Sure you can. Then think about the innocent harmless unborn babies. God put this voice in my head to speak for those who can't speak out for themselves. Shortly after I began writing about the voice I heard, I was notified that my granddaughter was pregnant and was planning to have an abortion. Could this have been the voice of my own great-granddaughter I heard speaking through to me? I believe so, through the power of God.

Chapter 3

God Worked It All Out

It was now about the last week in May, and I was still wondering how could I get my little story in print. When I came home from work, I began to wash the dishes. I heard the back door open and it was my son Kendrick. I fixed his plate and placed it on the table in front of him. As he began to eat, I noticed he didn't have that big appetite like he normally has, but I kept washing dishes. I was thinking maybe he had a bad day at work or something, but after a few minutes, I noticed he had almost stopped eating. Before I could say anything, he said in a distant voice, "Has Donna called you?"

I said, "No, why do you ask?"

He said, "I talked to her today and she said Bridget might be pregnant." Bridget is Kendrick and Donna's daughter.

For a moment, I just stood looking at him; he then pushed his plate back and said, "I don't know what I'm going to do."

I then said, "All we can do is pray, and God will work it out," but I was also praying that it wouldn't end in an abortion. I was hurt, my son was hurt, Donna was hurt, and my granddaughter was scared. I had not talked to Donna or Bridget, but I was praying that when I did talk to them, I could say the right thing to support them. Finally, one evening, I called Donna and asked her to ride with me to the grocery store, and she agreed. As we entered the store, she told me that Bridget was pregnant and she didn't want to keep the baby.

I said, "Oh lord, I don't believe in abortions." Donna said she didn't either, but Bridget said she wanted to finish school and she didn't think she could do it with a baby. I asked her if they had made any plans for the abortion arrangements, and she said they had to come up with some more money before they could do anything. I couldn't imagine my first great-grandchild not being born. I was praying that they didn't receive enough money to carry out the abortion. I knew I wasn't going to give them money; there was no way I would do such a thing. I continued to pray and pray and pray. Now this is when I had to go to my prayer closet and tell God all about it, not people. Later on, I talked to Donna and they almost had everything finalized. I had to go right back into my prayer closet and pray for this unborn baby girl: "Lord, please don't let them take her life; this is a painful way for any unborn child to die."

The next day after we had talked about abortion, I got a phone call from my son and he said, " You know, Bridget is supposed to have that abortion this week."

I said, "There's no way that will happen; I talked to a man this morning and he assured me that it wouldn't happen." I'm not sure if Kendrick knew who I was talking about, but the man's name is Jesus, and when Jehovah God says it's done, it's done. At the time, Bridget was around five months pregnant, so I called her to find out what was going on. When I began talking to Bridget, she told me she had already been up to the clinic, but one of the nurses told her she would have to come back because it would be a two-day procedure, but she didn't know that prayer had already changed all their plans. See, God is a good God—yes, he is—and I knew after praying sincerely to Jehovah God in the name of his son Jesus there was nothing that could make this abortion happen. No, it would not and could not happen; see, prayer is the key, and God is the answer. There's nothing to hard for God; see, God will give you the desires of your heart as long as you are sincere with him. One of my desires was to write a book that would be worthwhile. When I got serious with

11

God, he granted me that desire to write. God granted my desires to publish this book and to see my great-granddaughter. I just want to thank God for giving me those desires of my heart.

As my pastor, Robert Terrell, Jr., would always say, "Trust in the Lord and wait your time, but stay in line." Thank you for those inspiring words, pastor. The story ended beautifully; Bridget changed her mind about having the abortion. She graduated from high school, received a scholarship, and that has encouraged Bridget to attend medical school. On September 27, 2005, she delivered a beautiful baby girl named Tanayah. My prayers are answered.

Chapter 4

Calling All Ladies: Please Listen Up

To all of you ladies reading this book and poem, please visualize the little unborn baby begging for its life. Think about it as if you were on death row for no reason at all. How would you respond—wouldn't you want to know why? Just knowing that someone decided that they don't want you to live—how terrible would that be to you? Wouldn't you try to fight for your precious life? The innocent little babies can't speak for themselves, so God allowed me to hear this little voice, so it can touch the hearts of mankind. Ladies, you don't have to get an abortion; there are other options. You might say, "I'm not the one that's doing the killing" —oh, wait a minute, you're the one that's allowing it to happen. You are the one who is making the decision, so you are actually guilty. Please let this be a lesson to you, or if you know someone who is planning on having an abortion, tell her face to face that it's wrong. Just give her a copy of this book, or read the poem to her. A child is one of the most precious things on earth; would you throw your most precious jewelry away and never look back for it? Sure you wouldn't. Well, a child means so much more to us than jewelry. Remember that God loves you and God loves the unborn child, so why harm the harmless? You have sinned and done many things wrong, but if you are put on death row just because someone wanted you out of the way, think about how you would feel, the suffering and the pain you would go through before you die. Well, you could speak for yourself and express your feelings, right? This unborn child cannot speak for itself; that's why God has allowed this little voice to speak in my head through him, to be put into print for the unborn children. Let's work together, ladies; we can do it. If the reading of this book can change the heart and mind of just one person, then heaven will rejoice. Do you know what the scriptures say about the killing of the unborn? Let's pick up our Bibles for a moment: go to Psalm 139: 13-16. David was speaking to God. He said, "You formed my inward parts; you covered me in my mother's womb. I will praise you, for I am fearfully and wonderfully made, marvelous are your works and that my soul knows well." David said, "My frame was not hidden from you when I was made in secret." He told God, "Your eyes saw my substance being yet unformed and in your book they were all written. The days fashioned for me when, yet there were none of them." So as you can see, all the way back in biblical times, what David was saying was that God knew him from the time he was conceived and formed in his mother's womb, and God made him an individual physical being. So what I am saying is that even if you abort your baby shortly after you have conceived, God knows this is an individual physical being. So it's still not pleasing to God, whether abortions take place early in pregnancy or later; in God's sight it is wrong. Children are a blessing from God. Let's go back to the Old Testament for a moment, back in biblical times, and see what the punishment was for harming or killing an unborn child even if it was unintentionally. Let's go to the book of Exodus 21:22. It reads, "If men fight and hurt a woman with a child so that she gives birth prematurely yet no harm follows, he shall surely be punished according as the woman's husband imposes on him, and he shall pay as the judges determine." Now look at what the twenty-third verse says: "But if any harm follows," meaning if the baby is killed, "you shall give life for life." The penalty must match the crime; that was during biblical times, and as you can see, all the way back in the biblical time, there was punishment for killing babies. Throughout the years, there have been many people who have tried many ways to protect the unborn. I pray that one day soon we can come together nationwide and set aside the fifth Sunday in every month to send up special prayers to save our babies. Prayer is the key, and God is the answer.

Chapter 5

I Learned How to Lean and Depend on Jesus

As I said earlier in the book, it has been my desire from childhood to write. I have done a lot of writing, but I would just throw it away. I would do that because I didn't know anything about writing or publishing a book, and sometimes it's hard to get hooked up with the right people. I kept thinking about Oprah Winfrey, but I figured I couldn't get in touch with her. Then I remembered the old saying that I used to say and sing: "I learn how to lean and depend on Jesus; he's my friend and he's my guide. I found out if I trust him, he will provide."

Even though I'm much older now than I was when I first desired to write, I just kept praying to God through his son Jesus Christ. I was praying that he grant me the desire to write. It's forty something years later and God has worked it out for me. I kept asking people how to publish a book, but I didn't have much success with that. But I didn't give up, because I was trusting and leaning on Jesus. One Sunday, I was in church; this was in July, 2006, after I had finished my manuscript and just had it lying around the house. I was still praying to get my voice in print and a book on the shelf. I know this was inspiration from God; see, when you lean and depend on Jesus, he will see you through anything. On this particular Sunday, my pastor, Robert Terrell, was announcing the upcoming events, and he said that revival would be held on August fifth through the tenth. As he continued to speak, he also said that there would be a visitor here who had published some books. He said she would be here to sign books and to talk to anyone that wanted to talk to her. I thought to myself, this is what I need to get my story out there; this could be my big break. I said, "Lord, I know I work second shift and it is going to be very hard for me to get off without getting a point." I started to think and I realized I had a few more vacation days left, so I went to work on Monday and took Tuesday off. Tuesday, I was at revival, wondering who this person was. After service, someone said the author was in the fellowship hall, signing books. When I went to the fellowship hall, I saw a lady sitting there signing books, so I got in line and waited until it was my time. I asked this nice lady a few questions, and I found out she would be in town for the week. She told me the hotel where she was staying, and she gave me her phone number. The next morning, I drove down to the hotel and met her; she gave me a lot of information that was very helpful. I said, "Look at Jesus, stepping on in and working it all out." Remember that I learned how to lean and depend on Jesus; he's my friend, and he's my guide. After all the information, we again exchanged numbers to keep in touch. She called me later in the year and asked me if I had gotten the book published, and I said no, not yet.

She gave me some encouraging words; she said, "Go ahead and get it out there, because God is going to give you another book to write after this one."

I said, "Thank you for those encouraging words." I really believe that when God inspires you to do some-thing, you don't worry about how or why you should do it; just do it. If God inspires you to do something then he will give you what you need or who you need. This lady was a total stranger; I had never seen her before, but we connected like we had known each other all our lives. Someone asked me why I didn't write about abortions earlier in my life. I said it wasn't my time, but I stayed in line. God doesn't give you the desire of your heart by age, but by believing and trusting in him. I know I'm an older women now, but this is my time. There is a time for all things and this is my time. Blessings aren't just for the young or the old, the rich or the poor, the blacks or the whites, but for the believers in the Lord and savior Jesus Christ. Jesus is the only man that has walked the face of this earth that is everything you need, all in one man. If you will only believe and trust in him with all your heart, things will begin to go right in your life. To all the young ladies, please never ever think of having an abortion. God is not pleased with this; you can't go wrong when serving the lord, because he is lord of lords and king of kings, and when you make him lord of your life, that means you belongs to the king of kings. Isn't that good news? I've learned to lean and depend on Jesus for everything I need. When people mistreat you, just call the name Jesus; when you're at home, just call the name Jesus; when attitudes show up, just call the name Jesus; when people lie on you, just call the name Jesus; when you are not feeling well, just call the name Jesus. When I was writing this book, I was trusting and calling the name Jesus. He's my guide and he's my closest friend. At three o'clock in the morning, you can call on him, and do you know, you won't disturb him. When you can't find the words to pray, or you don't know what to say, just call the name of Jesus. Thanks to everyone who read this book. I pray that it will be beneficial to someone. If I hadn't been obedient and began to write as I was inspired, my manuscript would have still been in my room in the dresser drawer. So when God says do it, just do it. Don't ask questions; just do it.

Chapter 6

Mommy Please Don't Sentence Me to Die

Mommy, lying in your womb is my everyday bed; that is where I lay my little head. Through your body is the way I'm fed; why, Mommy, did you say what you said? You told your best friend you were pregnant with me, but I would be the little girl she would never see. Please, Mommy, don't sentence me to die.

I know I'm not fully developed yet, and my nostrils set apart, but I'm still the little unborn baby with a brain and a heart. Please, Mommy, don't sentence me to die.

My little body may be ugly to you now, and my ears seems out of place, but the pot didn't look good to the potter until it was finished with glaze.

When my little body is finish developing, I'll be such a beautiful child; please, Mommy, let me be born alive.

You have set the month, the day, and the hour; pray to God, Mommy; seek the highest power. Mommy, please let me live. I know it's in God's will. Please, Mommy, don't sentence me to die.

You have sentenced me now, Mommy, and you didn't even give me a name. Oh God, Mommy, what a shame. One day, Mommy, I could be the apple of your eye, and I promise, Mommy, I'll never make you cry. Please, Mommy, don't sentence me to die.

Mommy, I have never done anything wrong; please let me live to grow and be strong. Mommy, Grandma didn't give up on you; oh dear Mommy, I want to live, too. Please, Mommy, don't sentence me to die.

Mommy, you know I have never sinned; why do you want my life to end? Please, Mommy, don't sentence me to die. My little body will quiver with great pain; oh Mommy, what a shame. You will need me, Mommy, when you grow old; tell me, Mommy, how can you be so cold? Please, Mommy, don't sentence me to die.

If you don't want me for yourself, will you just give me to someone else? I will love you, Mommy, with all my heart. Why, Mommy, do we have to part? Please, Mommy, don't sentence me to die.

Mommy, if you just can't change your mind, I'll be with Jesus; I'll be just fine. Please, Mommy, if I have to die, bury my little body, but do not cry. Please, Mommy, don't sentence me to die.

Underneath the green grass is where I'll be, until Jesus comes and sets me free. Jesus will give me such a beautiful name, Mommy; you know what it will be. Read Mark 5: 41 and you will see. Please, Mommy, don't sentence me to die.

Mommy, I know the time has almost come, and it's almost the hour. I heard you praying, Mommy; you were seeking the highest power. You said, "Forgive me, father, it's not in your will to kill. Yes, God, yes, I want my little girl to live." Thank you, Mommy, for changing your mind; now it is time for a nap. I'm doing fine. I'll arrive in a few weeks, and awake from my nap; then my bed will be your lap. I'll be so cute living in your world; praise God, Mommy; I'm your baby girl. Thank you, Mommy, for taking me off death row; now I will live, laugh, play, and grow.

The Unborn
Author Doris Head

Words of Thanks

To the readers of this book, I wish to take this time to thank every one of you for taking the time to read my little book. Thanks to everyone that spoke encouraging words to me when I told them what my book was about. A great big thanks goes out to my granddaughters that helped me with editing my book. Thanks to my sons for the very sweet comments. Thanks to my supporters, and most of all, thank God for giving me this opportunity.

Doris Head

In loving memory of my son, Ricky Lewis Reid

About the Author

Born in Rutledge, Georgia, a small country town, from childhood until my adult years I have always spoken out for people. No matter what the situation is wheather they were shy or afraid to speak I was always out spoken, "as I was told". At a very young age I can remember speaking out for classmates and playmates. As I became older I began to speak out for sibling, co-workers, and friends. Just sitting back and watching people hurt and suffer because they don't have the courage to speak out just really hurts me. After been inspired to write about the unborn I'm now speaking out for those who don't have voices to speak out for themselves,(the precious unborn). I pray that the reading of this book and poem will allow you to hear the speaking of the unborn in print.

Author

Doris Head